TOP 10 POPULAR CHRISTMAS

10 of the Best-Loved Songs of the Season
Arranged in Jazz Styles for Late Intermediate to Early Advanced Pianists

Sharon Aaronson

The *Top 10 Popular Christmas* collection includes some of the most familiar Christmas songs that people enjoy year after year. Written during the 20th and early 21st centuries, these songs reappear with each generation, taking on new life in a diversity of styles. Judy Garland introduced "Have Yourself a Merry Little Christmas" in 1944, and that song has since been recorded by countless artists as diverse as Ella Fitzgerald, James Taylor, and Christina Aguilera. Originally made famous by Eartha Kitt in 1953, "Santa Baby" continued to be recorded by many performers including Madonna and Taylor Swift. Most recently, in 2004 Josh Groban's exquisite voice was heard singing the hit "Believe" on the soundtrack of the animated feature film *The Polar Express*. While the list of performers and genres is vast, these songs all share a common thread as they signal the arrival of Christmas and the joy of sharing the season with family and friends. May all of you have a very Merry Christmas and Happy New Year!

Sharon Aaronson

to Leah & Charlie, and Mara & Kevin, with love

Produced by
Alfred Music Publishing Co., Inc.
P.O. Box 10003
Van Nuys, CA 91410-0003
alfred.com

Printed in USA.

ISBN-10: 0-7390-8139-X
ISBN-13: 978-0-7390-8139-6

The Christmas Waltz

Words by Sammy Cahn
Music by Jule Styne
Arr. by Sharon Aaronson

Have Yourself a Merry Little Christmas

Words and Music by
Hugh Martin and Ralph Blane
Arr. by Sharon Aaronson

Slowly and expressively

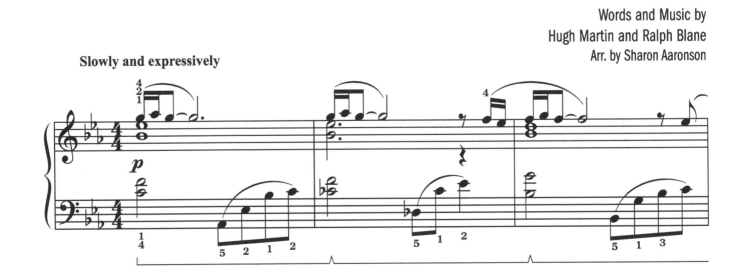

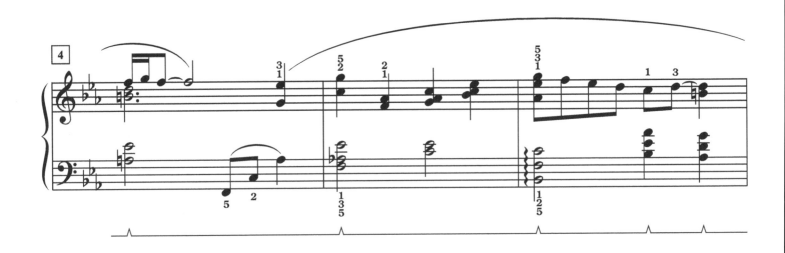

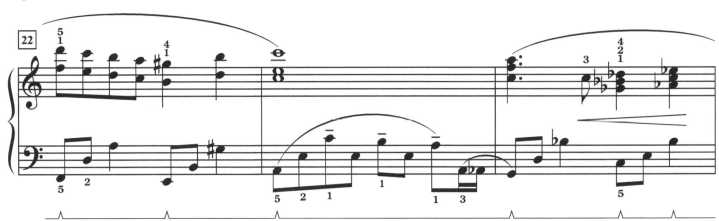

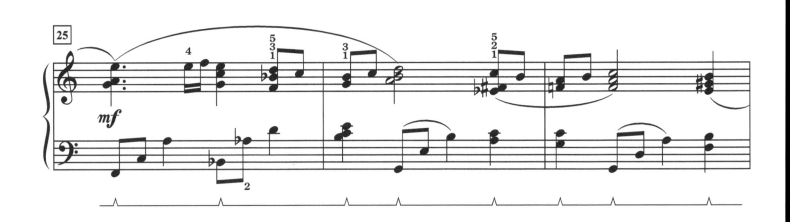

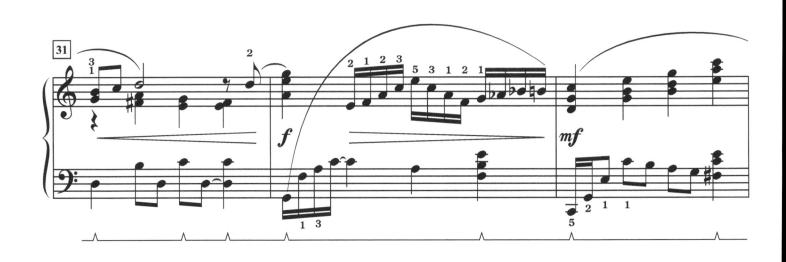

Santa Baby

Words and Music by
Joan Javits, Philip Springer and Tony Springer
Arr. by Sharon Aaronson

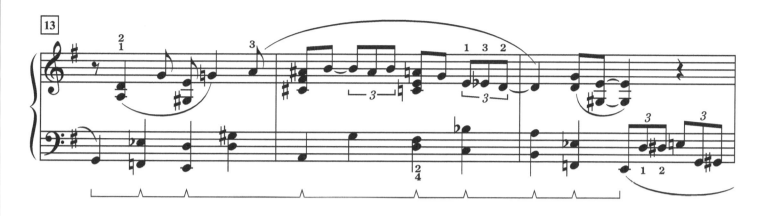

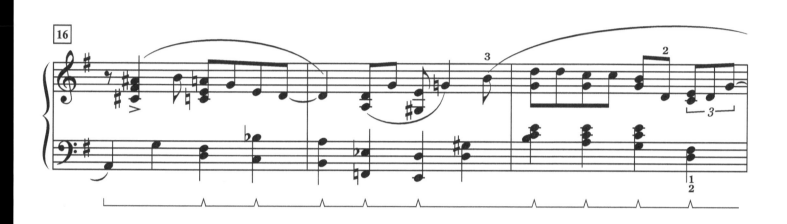

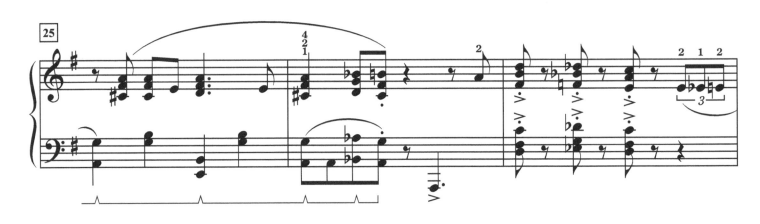

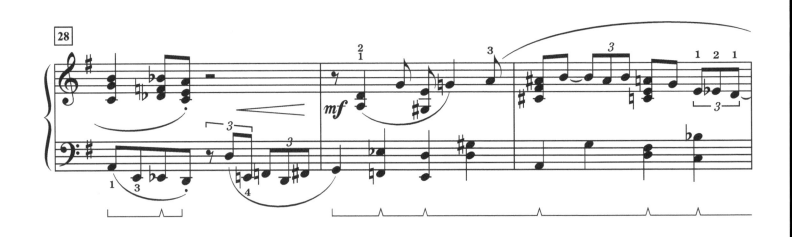

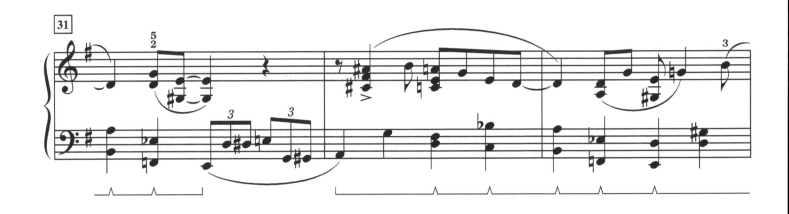

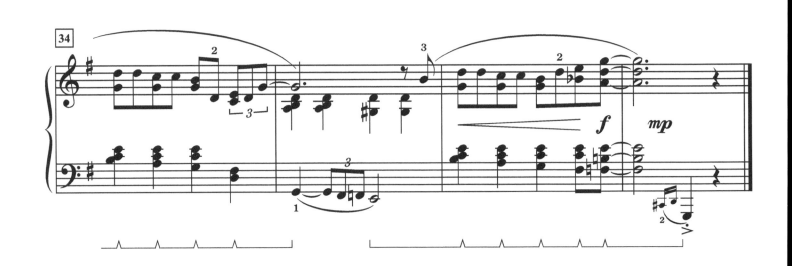

Believe

(from *The Polar Express*)

Words and Music by Alan Silvestri and Glen Ballard
Arr. by Sharon Aaronson

It's the Most Wonderful Time of the Year

Words and Music by
Eddie Pola and George Wyle
Arr. by Sharon Aaronson

*Play straight eighths in measures 18–19, 39–40, and 77–79.

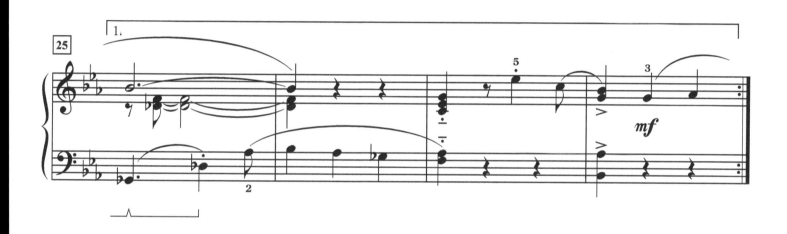

Let It Snow! Let It Snow! Let It Snow!

Words by Sammy Cahn
Music by Jule Styne
Arr. by Sharon Aaronson

I'll Be Home for Christmas

Words by Kim Gannon
Music by Walter Kent
Arr. by Sharon Aaronson

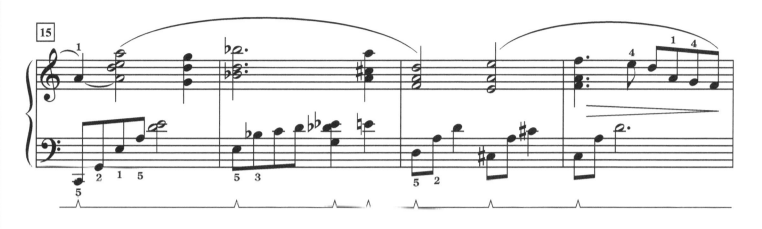

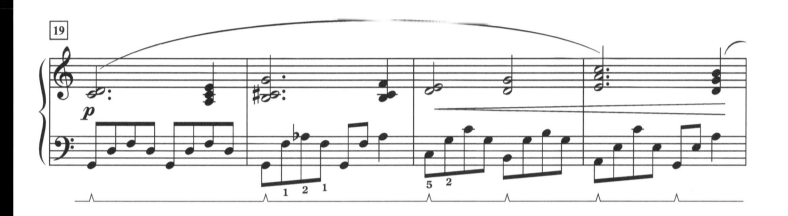

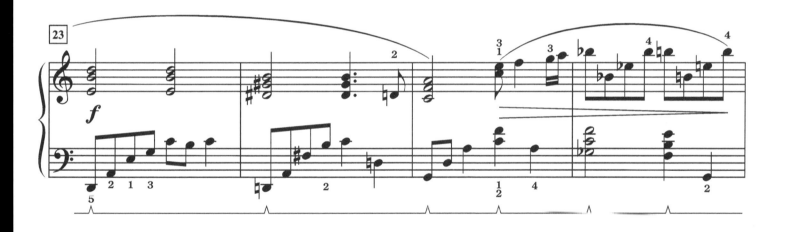

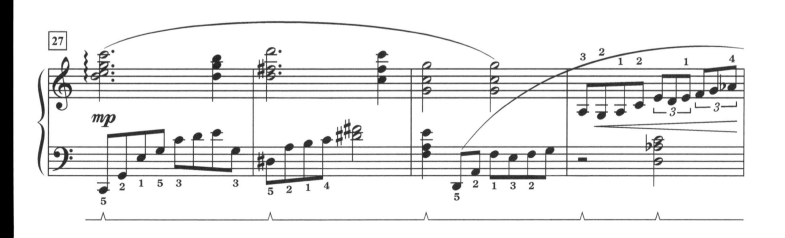

Winter Wonderland

Words by Dick Smith
Music by Felix Bernard
Arr. by Sharon Aaronson

The Little Drummer Boy

Words and Music by
Harry Simeone, Henry Onorati and Katherine Davis
Arr. by Sharon Aaronson

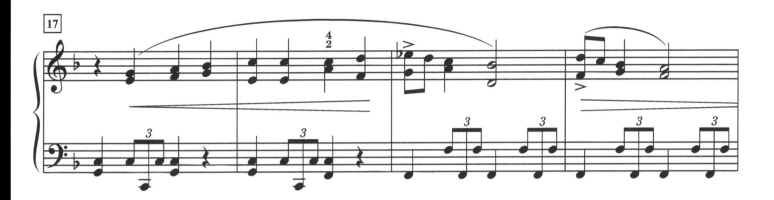

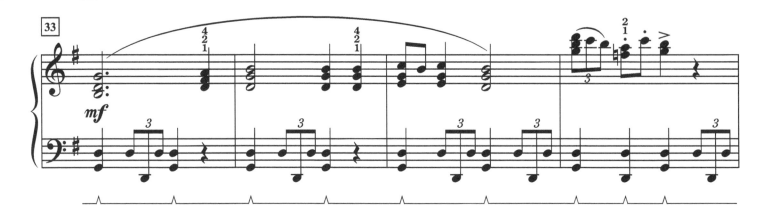

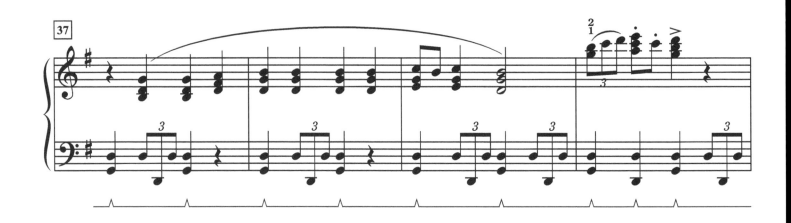

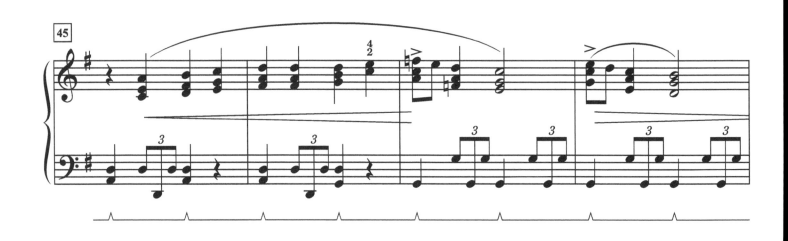

Sleigh Ride

By Leroy Anderson
Arr. by Sharon Aaronson

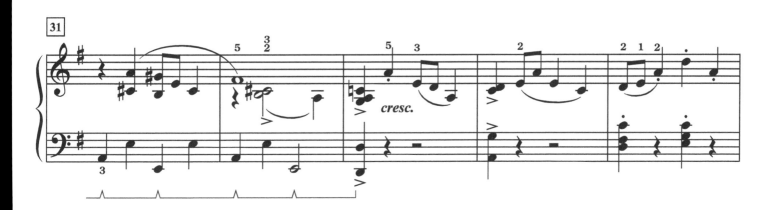

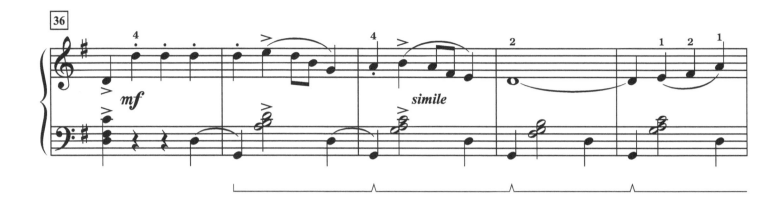

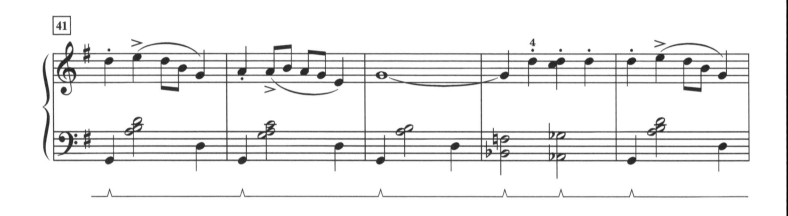

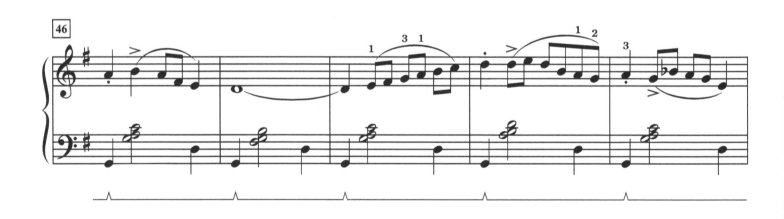

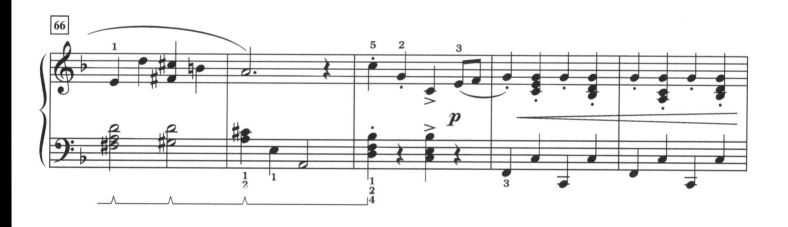

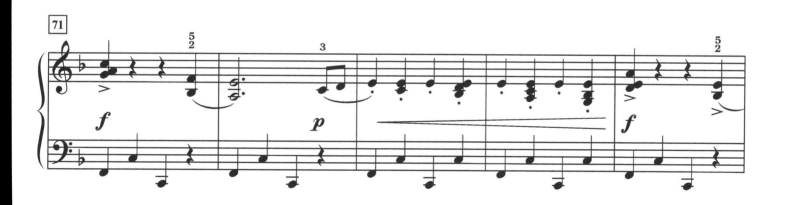

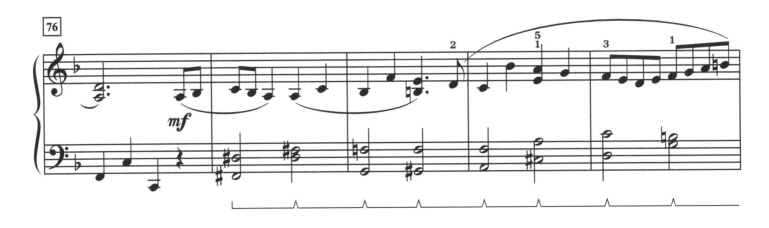

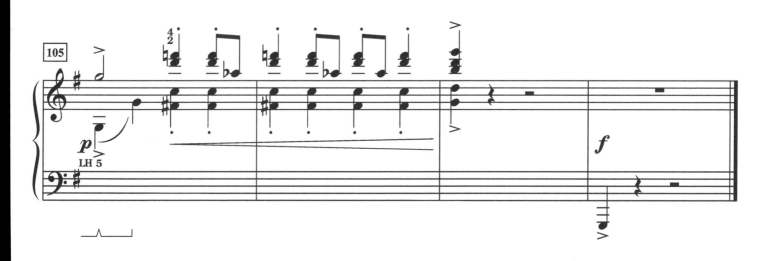